Medicine

Paul Dowswell

nn
Y

www.heinemann.co.uk/library
Visit our website to find out more information about Heinemann Library books.

To order:
☎ Phone 44 (0) 1865 888066
🖹 Send a fax to 44 (0) 1865 314091
💻 Visit the Heinemann Bookshop at www.heinemann.co.uk/library to browse our catalogue and order online.

First published in Great Britain by Heinemann Library, Halley Court, Jordan Hill, Oxford OX2 8EJ, a division of Reed Educational and Professional Publishing Ltd. Heinemann is a registered trademark of Reed Educational & Professional Publishing Limited.

OXFORD MELBOURNE AUCKLAND JOHANNESBURG BLANTYRE
GABORONE IBADAN PORTSMOUTH NH (USA) CHICAGO

Designed by Tinstar Design (www.tinstar.co.uk)
Illustrations by Martin Griffin
Originated by Ambassador Litho Ltd
Printed by Wing King Tong in Hong Kong/China

ISBN 0431 13230 5 (hardback)   ISBN 0431 13235 6 (paperback)
06 05 04 03 02 01   06 05 04 03 02
10 9 8 7 6 5 4 3 2 1   10 9 8 7 6 5 4 3 2 1

British Library Cataloguing in Publication Data
Dowswell, Paul
      Medicine. – (Great Inventions)
      1. Medicine – History
      I. Title
      610.9

Acknowledgements
The Publishers would like to thank the following for permission to reproduce photographs: AKG pp12, 30, Bridgeman Art Library p4, Corbis p8, Marconi Ltd p32, Mary Evans Picture Library p16, Michael Holford p6, National Medical Slide Bank p7, Science and Society Picture Library pp9, 10, 15, 18, 25, 28, 34, Science Photo Library pp5, 13, 20 21 (John Greim), 22 (Brooks and Brown), 35, 37, 38 (Scott Camazine), 40, 41 (Simon Fraser), 42, 43, TP Orthodontics Inc p27, The Wellcome Centre Photolibrary p39.

Cover photograph reproduced with permission of Imagebank and Photodisc.

Every effort has been made to contact copyright holders of any material reproduced in this book. Any omissions will be rectified in subsequent printings if notice is given to the Publisher.

Any words appearing in the text in bold, **like this**, are explained in the Glossary.

Contents

Introduction

Medicine is the art of preventing and treating disease and injury. It is an area rich in invention. Some of these inventions, such as X-rays and stethoscopes, have made a major contribution to saving lives and relieving pain. Others, such as false teeth and hearing aids, have just made life more comfortable and convenient for people.

Humans have been practising medicine since prehistoric times, but for most of history the treatments doctors inflicted on their patients were just as likely to kill them as cure them. The first surgical instruments were invented to perform a gruesome operation called **trepanning**, where holes were drilled into the skull of a patient. The idea of this procedure was to release the evil spirits that were thought to be causing their illness.

Key invention

Once doctors began to understand the causes of sickness, they could set about curing it much more effectively. Some of medicine's greatest discoveries have been made possible by the invention of the microscope. Light microscopes were invented in the late 16th century. They allowed scientists to look into a previously invisible world and discover **bacteria**, some of the most important causes of disease and infection. The invention of the electron microscope in the 20th century led to the discovery of **viruses**. Electron microscopes also allowed researchers to unlock the secrets of our **genes**. They showed how the minuscule chemical mechanisms of **DNA** can carry inherited illnesses from parent to child. The new science of **genetic engineering** promises to revolutionize medicine and provide a whole host of extraordinary cures.

Medicine in the early 13th century. As a surgeon operates on a growth on his nose, the poor patient has to hold a basin to catch his blood. Until Victorian times, when anaesthetics and antiseptics were invented, surgery was an agonizing and often fatal business.

Seeing through you

Some inventions have been put to use almost immediately. Wilhelm Roentgen's X-ray machine made headlines around the world within weeks of its development in 1895. It quickly became a common sight in hospitals. On the other hand, the **anaesthetic** qualities of some gases were known about for 50 years before anyone thought to use them to save patients from the agony of surgery.

Today, many of the miracles of modern medicine are so commonplace that it is easy to take them for granted. MRI and ultrasound scanners use magnetic fields and sound waves to allow doctors to see beneath our skin in an instant. They detect **tumours** without the need for exploratory surgery, and monitor the health of a baby in the womb with minimal inconvenience for the mother-to-be. Even when surgery is inevitable, many operations can be performed with only the tiniest incisions, thanks to **fibre-optic** technology. This enables surgeons to see and manipulate tiny surgical instruments inside the body.

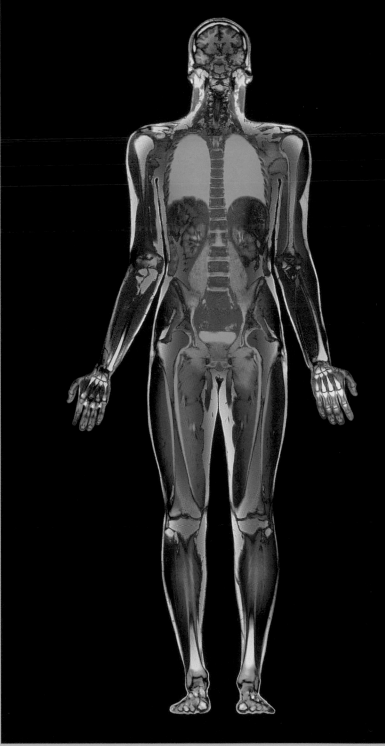

*Over the past 100 years several inventions have made it possible for doctors to see inside the body of a patient. This extraordinary image is a whole-body MRI scan. The skeleton is clearly visible (in orange), as are **organs** such as the lungs (in green).*

Scalpel, c. 3000BC

Surgery is one of the earliest kinds of medicine known to humankind. So it is fitting that the scalpel should be the first invention in this book. A scalpel is a small, light and very sharp knife. It is one of the surgeon's most essential tools. It has a small, but extremely effective blade, and is ideal for delicate and precise **incisions**.

Scalpels were not the first surgical instruments. These were simple stones, usually flint or obsidian, chiselled into shape by other, harder stones. The earliest ones we know of date from about 10,000BC.

Bodies in Stone Age burial sites show clear evidence of surgery. Bone-setting and amputations show that early humans nursed their wounded back to health. Neat, round holes in the skulls of some bodies show that an appalling surgical procedure called **trepanning** took place.

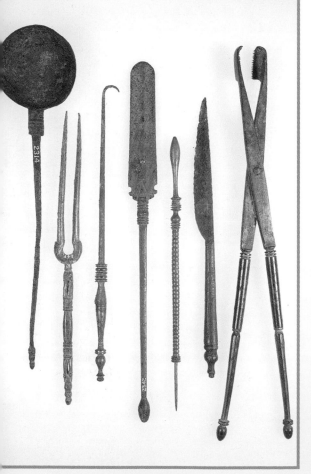

A collection of medical instruments from Ancient Rome. The knife-like instrument is easy to pick out as the scalpel – which has changed little over the centuries.

Ancient instruments

Evidence of the first known surgical tools, including a scalpel-like bronze knife, have been found among Sumerian archaeological remains dating from around 3000BC. (This area is now modern Iraq.) Early civilizations, from the Egyptians to the Greeks and Romans, went on to invent more recognizable surgical tools. Surviving paintings, carvings and other artefacts show medical instruments of surprising delicacy and sophistication. Carved from bone or wood, or cast in iron or bronze, they would change little over the next 40 centuries.

As ancient civilizations developed their metalwork skills, so their scalpels and other surgical instruments became more refined. Medical equipment preserved in the volcanic ash of Pompeii includes tools of great delicacy, many of which would look familiar to surgeons today. There are forceps, probes and amputation blades

as well as scalpels. Their handles are bronze and have indentations to increase the surgeon's grip. At either end is a blade made from iron. Surgeons preferred this metal as it was more hard-wearing than bronze or copper, and could be sharpened more effectively.

Scalpels from these times would have been used for a variety of surgical procedures. Egyptian surgeons, for example, removed **abscesses** and **tumours**. In India, cataracts (a cloudy lens in the eye) and bladder stones were removed with great skill. Surgeons from all these civilizations also treated wounded soldiers. Surgery has always involved cutting, snipping, delving and sewing, and the tools that do this have changed little over the centuries.

The scalpel has been one of the surgeon's most effective tools for five thousand years. Only time will tell if the laser beam will make it obsolete.

Modern tools

Modern surgeons have another cutting instrument undreamed of by their predecessors – the **laser** beam. This can cut through skin or **organ** tissue in microseconds, and with a precision that even the finest scalpel-wielding surgeon would be unable to match. Lasers are particularly useful for delicate eye operations.

In the future, scalpels and surgeons may even part company. Robot arms may wield these cutting tools. Surgeons connected to their patients via video screens and Internet links, may perform life-saving operations on accident victims or battle casualties, hundreds or even thousands of miles away.

c. 10,000BC	c. 3000BC	c. AD 50	1962
FIRST EVIDENCE OF SURGERY	SUMERIANS DEVELOP COPPER SCALPEL SURGICAL INSTRUMENTS	ROMANS USE SCALPELS WITH BRONZE HANDLES AND HARD-WEARING IRON BLADES	LASER FIRST USED IN SURGERY

Acupuncture needles, c. 2000BC

Almost all the techniques and ideas of modern medicine can be rationally explained. We know that pain, for example, is caused by stimulation of a nerve ending that sends a signal in the form of an electrical impulse to the brain. Chinese medicine, however, provides at least one major technique that western knowledge of the human body cannot explain. Indeed, there seems to be something almost magical about acupuncture's ability to stop pain and cure illness.

How does it work?

In acupuncture, needles are stuck into specific points along the body. The Chinese call them 'meridian points', and there are 360 in total. The traditional Chinese explanation for acupuncture is that energy flows along lines in the body connecting these points. If that flow of energy is interrupted, illness follows. Inserting and twirling needles in meridian points causes the energy to flow again and heals the patient.

Acupuncture involves the use of special needles. These were first invented around 2000BC and were slivers of stone, but bronze, gold and silver needles were also made in Ancient China. As well as curing such ailments as **rheumatism** and heart disease, acupuncture can be used as an **anaesthetic** during an operation.

A traditional set of acupuncture needles. In most acupuncture treatments there are nine needles, each of which has a different shape and use.

Out of favour

When Europeans began to arrive in China in the late 18th and early 19th centuries, the Chinese were greatly impressed with their medical theories and techniques. Acupuncture fell out of fashion and for a while it was even banned.

However, acupuncturists practised their art in secret and now it has made a comeback. It is widely used in China, not only as an anaesthetic, but also to treat heart disease, **ulcers**, high blood pressure, **asthma** and other ailments. Many modern doctors recognize its benefits. Acupuncture is available in most developed countries and has even been used to treat mental illness.

Electric needles

Acupuncture has moved with the times. Needles are now made of stainless steel, which is more hygienic. Instead of twirling them to encourage energy flow, many acupuncturists send electric current through the needles, which seems to do the job just as effectively. Scientists are still puzzled about how acupuncture actually works. Some **sceptics** suggest that the needles are effective because the patient believes they will work but acupuncturists have used their methods on animals with equally effective results. Another explanation offered is that the needles cause the body to release natural painkillers called enkephalins and endorphins into the bloodstream. These block the pathways of pain signals on the way to the brain. Although this is yet to be proven, it seems to be the most likely explanation for how this extraordinary Chinese technique works.

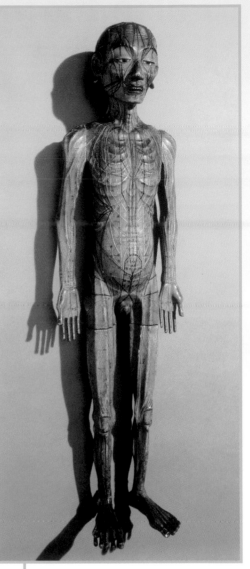

This extraordinary 17th-century wooden figure was made as a teaching aid for student acupuncturists. The lines along the figure show the direction and flow of energy in the body. Along the lines are 360 'meridian points' where acupuncture needles can be inserted.

c. 2000BC	**1822**	**1949 ONWARDS**	**1970s ONWARDS**
FIRST KNOWN USE OF ACUPUNCTURE NEEDLES	ACUPUNCTURE OFFICIALLY BANNED, AS WESTERN MEDICINE BECOMES POPULAR IN CHINA	COMMUNIST TAKE-OVER OF CHINA. ACUPUNCTURE OFFICIALLY ENCOURAGED	USE OF ACUPUNCTURE SPREADS TO THE WEST AND IS GRADUALLY ACCEPTED BY WESTERN MEDICAL AUTHORITIES

False teeth, c. 700BC

Given that eating is such an essential part of human life, and tooth decay and loss has been a problem from the earliest times, it is surprising that it took so long for anyone to come up with the idea of false teeth.

The first ones we know of were invented by the Etruscans – a culture that flourished in southern Italy before being conquered by the Romans. False teeth with gold bridgework (clamps) to attach them to healthy teeth have been found in Etruscan tombs. They date from around 700BC. The teeth were carved from ivory or bone, or were second-hand human teeth.

Amazingly, there were no further advances in dentistry for the next 2500 years. Human teeth were always in plentiful supply, especially after a war. Ivory teeth, too, continued to be used but these rotted and turned green as regularly as real teeth did. They also tasted horrible and were expensive to replace.

Made to last

In 1770 a French chemist named Alexis Duchâteau invented porcelain false teeth, which immediately became popular. They were life-like and easy to clean, did not rot nor leave a horrible taste in the mouth. On top of all that, they were cheap. A hundred years later, advances in rubber production allowed porcelain teeth to be mounted on a

The world's first false teeth. These gold and ivory dentures date from around 700BC.

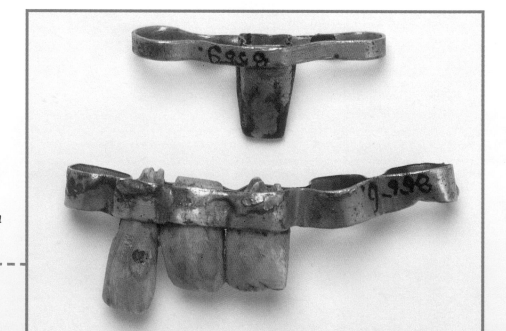

10

rubber plate that could be moulded to fit the shape of the patient's mouth. Over the last century false teeth have increasingly been made from plastics such as acrylic resin. This has made them even cheaper, stronger, lighter and easier to clean.

Although false teeth allow wearers to speak and eat as though they have real teeth, they are still an uncomfortable inconvenience. Today, those who can afford the considerable expense, can have a full set of false teeth implants. In a procedure unimaginable before the invention of **anaesthetics**, screws are drilled into the jaw-bone and the new teeth are set into the gum.

The dentist's drill

Around the 1st century AD doctors realized that rotting teeth did not always have to be removed. If there was only minor decay it could be treated by drilling it out. This was always going to be difficult, as teeth are made of enamel – the hardest substance in the body.

The first known drill was used by a Roman surgeon named Archigenes around AD 100. It was powered by a rope, and must have been fearfully painful for the patient. Later drills were powered by a flywheel turned by a foot pedal, and even clockwork.

Speed is an essential part of reducing the discomfort of drilling. Today, drills are powered by air **turbines** and revolve at an extraordinary 200,000 revolutions a minute. They are also water-cooled to reduce the heat generated by such high-speed contact with a tooth.

c. 700BC	1770	1851	1935
FIRST KNOWN FALSE TEETH	PORCELAIN FALSE TEETH INVENTED	RUBBER PLATES MAKE FALSE TEETH MORE COMFORTABLE TO WEAR	PLASTIC FALSE TEETH INTRODUCED

Artificial limbs, AD 1536

One of Paré's more ingenious artificial hands. This cutaway engraving shows the gears and levers that worked the fingers. It is taken from Paré's book of his works, Oeuvres, which was published in 1575.

Wounds from wild animals or warfare are often fatal but sometimes a hunter or a soldier may suffer an injury as terrible as the loss of a limb and still survive. There is evidence that this happened to the earliest human cave-dwellers. The fact that the wound had time to heal shows that these people were willing to look after their invalid fellow humans, even though their use to a tribe would be severely limited.

Humankind's use of tools set them aside from other creatures, even two million years ago. It was a natural step to begin using strap-on sticks and hooks as replacement legs or arms. Greek historian Herodotus wrote about a man with a wooden foot in 500BC. Roman mosaics feature men with peg legs but it was not until the 16th century that the first proper artificial limbs were made. They were invented by an extraordinary French army surgeon named Ambroise Paré. Making use of the intricate metalwork techniques mastered by makers of armour, he began in 1536 to make legs and arms from iron and leather. Some even had **gears** and **levers** to simulate the movement of fingers.

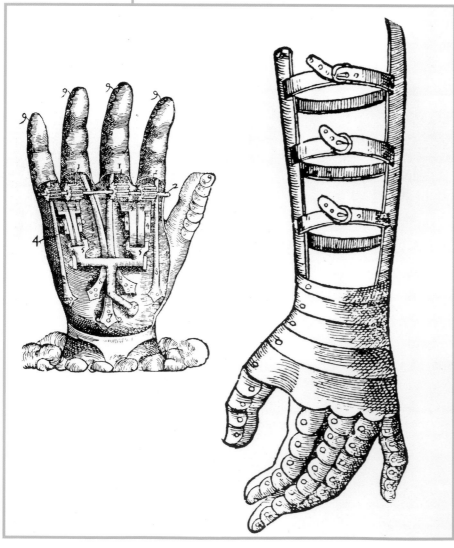

Prosthetics

Paré's work laid the foundations of prosthetics – a branch of surgery concerned with artificial limbs and other **organs** such as eyeballs. Today, the most advanced artificial limbs are ingenious, complex devices. Known as myoelectric limbs, they work in the same way as human limbs – reacting to nerve impulses from the brain that tell them to move. Today, people who have lost arms or legs can dance, run and even ski, in a way that would have made Paré and his patients gasp in envy and astonishment.

Ambroise Paré (1517–90)

Paré learned his trade as a barber-surgeon – the lowest rank of the medical profession in 16th-century Europe. Such men would cut hair and shave customers, as well as perform major operations, seal wounds with boiling oil and lance **abscesses**. This was all work too dirty and unpleasant for the higher-class doctors. Although he was highly intelligent, Paré was forced to enter medicine in this way because he had a poor education and was not able to learn the Latin and Greek necessary to study medicine at university.

As well as inventing artificial limbs, Paré also pioneered the technique of treating wounds with ointments. He invented ingenious surgical instruments and rose to become the surgeon to four kings of France. Once, when being praised for saving a patient he said, 'I treated him and God healed him', words that would later be engraved on his tombstone.

*Surgery in Paré's time. This soldier is having his leg amputated by an army surgeon. There was no **anaesthetic** and he has been blindfolded to prevent him seeing what is going on.*

500BC	1536	1575	1990s
FIRST RECORDED REFERENCE TO ARTIFICIAL LIMB, BY GREEK HISTORIAN HERODOTUS	AMBROISE PARÉ BEGINS TO MAKE ARTIFICIAL LIMBS	PARÉS BOOK *OEUVRES*, DETAILING HIS EXPERIENCES AS A SURGEON, IS PUBLISHED	MYOELECTRIC LIMBS, REACTING TO NERVE IMPULSES, DEVELOPED

Microscope, c. 1590

Today we all know that illness is caused by germs – tiny **bacteria** and **viruses** – which attack our body and make us feel poorly. Until the microscope was invented, however, the tiny world of bacteria and viruses was one that could not even be imagined, let alone studied.

The most important ingredient in a microscope is a **lens** – a piece of curved glass that magnifies (makes bigger) whatever is seen through it. People in the earliest civilizations must have observed how a blob of water or bead of glass can make things look bigger. By the 13th century, glass-makers had applied this knowledge to make glass lenses that could be used as spectacles to correct poor eyesight. Lenses always inspired superstitious mistrust among the people of medieval Europe. Anything that could not be easily understood was often dismissed as sorcery. It was not until the late 16th century that it occurred to anybody to use a lens to study small things.

Blurred image

Like the telescope (which uses the same basic principle), the microscope seemed to be invented in several places at once. Most historians agree that it was Zacharias Jansen who made the first microscope, in 1590. Jansen was a spectacle-maker from Middelburg, Holland. His device magnified objects about nine times and showed a rather blurred image. Jansen made little use of his invention. After all, as many people reasoned at the time, what was the point in looking at small things? Fortunately for science, there were more inquisitive minds around. They took up Jansen's invention, improved it, and went on to make some of the most significant discoveries in human history.

Leeuwenhoek's microscope

In the century after Jansen's original invention, a Dutchman named Antoni van Leeuwenhoek was making his own primitive microscopes.

This 17th-century microscope was owned by English scientist Robert Hooke. In Hooke's time, gentlemen would keep a microscope among the gold-embossed books in their library. This microscope's fine leather and wood appearance was intended to fit in with such a setting.

A linen merchant by trade, he had originally developed his microscope to study the quality of the cloth he bought. His device used only a single lens, but it could magnify up to 200 times. Leeuwenhoek was not an educated man, but he was endlessly inquisitive. He used his device to unearth a microworld previously undreamed of.

'Animalcules'

Leeuwenhoek discovered sperm and studied the structure of muscles, eyes, arteries and veins. He made his most important discovery when examining a speck of plaque which he had scraped from his teeth. It seemed to be made up of thousands of tiny wriggling creatures, which he called 'animalcules'. What Leeuwenhoek had seen were bacteria.

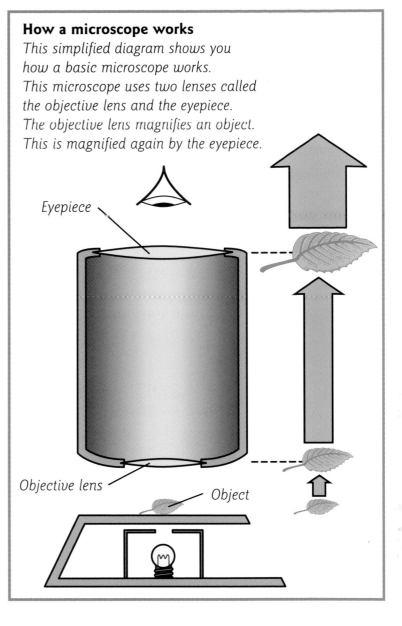

How a microscope works
This simplified diagram shows you how a basic microscope works. This microscope uses two lenses called the objective lens and the eyepiece. The objective lens magnifies an object. This is magnified again by the eyepiece.

Eyepiece

Objective lens

Object

Other, more trained scientific minds, would go on to make the connection between 'animalcules' and illness. Nevertheless Leeuwenhoek had used his microscope to take humankind's first real steps in our understanding of the causes of illness. Over the next four centuries the microscope would prove to be the most invaluable tool in the fight against disease.

13TH CENTURY	1590	1665	1668	1830	1861
FIRST SPECTACLES MADE FROM GLASS LENSES	ZACHARIAS JANSEN MAKES FIRST MICROSCOPE	ROBERT HOOKE PUBLISHES *MICROGRAPHIA* – A BOOK OF 'DESCRIPTIONS OF MINUTE BODIES MADE BY MAGNIFYING GLASSES'	FIRST RECORDED USE OF MICROSCOPE BY ANTONI VAN LEEUWENHOEK	JOSEPH LISTER MAKES MICROSCOPE WITH IMPROVED LENSES, WHICH CAN MAGNIFY 2000 TIMES	LOUIS PASTEUR USES A MICROSCOPE TO PROVE THAT BACTERIA CAUSE ILLNESS

Blood transfusion, 1667

Loss of blood is one of the major causes of death following an accident or surgery. Replacing it with blood from other humans seems like an obvious idea but it was not until the early 17th century that this was first attempted.

As with many inventions in history, there is confusion about who first carried out a blood transfusion. English physician Richard Lower performed successful dog-to-dog transfusions in 1665, but some medical documents mention transfusions as early as 1630. Most people agree, though, that Jean-Baptiste Denis was the first man to carry out a transfusion on a human being. Curiously, rather than taking blood from another person, he used a lamb. This was because he had had success with previous animal-to-animal transfusions.

In this 17th-century engraving a man is transferring blood from a cow to his own body. Such animal-to-human transfusions often caused nausea and diarrhoea and were sometimes fatal.

Short-lived success

Denis was Professor of Philosophy and Mathematics at the University of Montpellier, France. In 1667, when he was presented with a 15-year-old boy who was suffering from acute lethargy and fever, he thought a transfusion of fresh blood may offer a cure. Amazingly, the transfusion was a success. Apart from feeling a great sensation of heat in his arm during the process, Denis's patient made a remarkable recovery, regaining his previous energy and appetite for life.

Denis's success however was an inexplicable fluke. Subsequently most people given animal blood suffered terrible effects. If they were lucky, they were sick. If they were unlucky, they died. These frightening failures convinced Denis he was on the wrong track. They also led to laws being passed forbidding animal-human transfusions and, for the moment, experimentation stopped.

Denis's failures seemed to indicate that human-to-human blood transfusion might be more successful although this, too, was an extremely dangerous process. Throughout the 19th century, physicians were constantly puzzled by the hit-and-miss nature of blood transfusions. For no apparent reason some patients died and some recovered.

Blood grouping

An Austrian physician, Karl Landsteiner, provided the answer. In 1901 he discovered that all human blood was not the same. He suggested there were three basic types – known as A, B and O. We now know there is a fourth main type, AB. Landsteiner realized that only some blood types were compatible. Those that were not acted against each other, causing the body to reject the new blood it had been given.

Once this hurdle had been overcome, the way was clear for widespread use of blood transfusions. During the Second World War they became commonplace, and saved countless lives.

Today, blood can be given directly to patients via plastic blood bags, which are far less likely to shatter or break than the previously used glass bottles. Most countries have a system of collecting blood through volunteer donors, and particular chemicals are used to keep the blood fresh and ready for use.

Recipe for blood
Blood is made up of several ingredients. Red blood **cells** carry oxygen around the body, white blood cells and platelets fight infections, and all of these float around in a liquid called plasma.

1630s	1665	1667	1818	1901	1932
FIRST MENTION OF BLOOD TRANSFUSIONS IN MEDICAL RECORDS	SUCCESSFUL DOG-TO-DOG TRANSFUSION PERFORMED	FIRST SUCCESSFUL ANIMAL-TO-HUMAN TRANSFUSION BY JEAN-BAPTISTE DENIS	FIRST SUCCESSFUL HUMAN-TO-HUMAN TRANSFUSION BY JAMES BLUNDELL	KARL LANDSTEINER DISCOVERS 'BLOOD GROUP' TYPES	FIRST BLOOD BANK SET UP, IN LENINGRAD, RUSSIA

Stethoscope, 1819

The stethoscope is such a simple and useful tool, it is a wonder that it took so long to invent. It allows a doctor to listen clearly to the movement of blood in the heart, air in the lungs and gases in the stomach and gut. Despite its simple design, it has proved to be one of the most useful medical inventions of all time and is still a vital tool for the modern doctor.

A French doctor named René-Théophile-Hyacinthe Laënnec was the first physician to realize that a tube would make it easier to listen to body fluids. He was a specialist in heart and lung diseases, and the noises such diseases produce are vital clues to their presence in the body.

Paper tube

One story says that Laënnec saw two boys playing with a wooden pole in the courtyard of the Louvre Palace in Paris. As one boy placed his ear to one end of the pole, the other boy scratched at the opposite end with a nail. Some time later, in 1819, Laënnec was examining a woman patient who he suspected had a heart problem. He needed to listen to her heart but in those days it was felt to be indecent for a doctor to place his head on a woman's chest. Laënnec remembered the two boys and their pole. He rolled a piece of paper into a tube and placed this against her heart. He was delighted to realize that he could hear so much more clearly. He soon found he could hear even better when he used a hollow wooden cylinder.

Laënnec's wooden cylinder stethoscope. Barely more complex than a rolled-up piece of paper, it proved to be one of the most essential medical tools ever invented.

Improved designs

Laënnec improved the design and the first widely used stethoscope was around 23 centimetres long and unscrewed in half so it could be carried in the pocket. It had a bell-like chamber at the 'patient end' which helped to pick up the body's internal noises. Distinct gasps and gurgles, for example, told a doctor whether their patient had such serious ailments as **bronchitis**, **pneumonia** or **tuberculosis**. In a cruel twist of fate Laënnec himself died of tuberculosis aged only 45. The stethoscope we know today was designed in 1855 by an American doctor named George Philip Cammann. He took Laënnec's basic idea and improved it. Inside the bell-shaped chamber he added a **diaphragm**, which picked up more sounds. The chamber was connected to two earpieces (for stereo sound) via a y-shaped rubber tube. Next time you visit a doctor, you will see that this design has stayed essentially the same for 150 years.

Better diagnosis

Diagnosis means the identification of a disease through looking at its signs and symptoms. In Laënnec's time diagnosis was difficult. It was thought improper for doctors to touch their patients, apart from taking their pulse and maybe tapping their back to listen for fluid on the lungs. Instead, the patient would tell the doctor their medical history, and the doctor would make his diagnosis by what he could see, hear and smell.

Laënnec, and other physicians in Paris – one of the great medical centres of early 19th-century Europe – realized that a more 'hands-on' approach to medicine was essential. The stethoscope helped in this but without involving the doctor making direct physical contact. It took an entire century for the stethoscope to be accepted however, both by patients and their doctors. Queen Victoria, for example, refused to allow a doctor to use one on her.

1819	1822	1855
FIRST USE OF STETHOSCOPE BY LAËNNEC	LAËNNEC APPOINTED AS PROFESSOR AT THE COLLEGÈ DE FRANCE	USING LAËNNEC'S IDEA, AMERICAN DOCTOR GEORGE PHILIP CAMMANN DESIGNS THE MODERN STETHOSCOPE WITH TWO EARPIECES

Anaesthetic inhaler, 1845

Today we think of pain as something that can be avoided. Most painful illnesses and injuries can be soothed by drugs. Agonizing medical processes and procedures can be made bearable by **anaesthetics** – chemicals which deaden pain. The word 'anaesthetic' is derived from a Greek word meaning 'loss of feeling'.

Anaesthetics have only been with us since the mid-19th century. Before then, patients unlucky enough to undergo surgery were strapped to an operating table and held down by strong men. Their screams and writhing cannot have helped the surgeon, who would be judged as much for the speed of his work as for his skill.

From the earliest times, doctors all over the world sought to discover methods to relieve the pain of surgery. In China, acupuncture was so effective it is still used today. Elsewhere, narcotic drugs, hypnosis and stupefying amounts of alcohol all had some limited use.

This is what 19th century anaesthetic equipment looked like. The glass jar contains sponges soaked in ether, and a tube connected to a rubber mask to allow a patient to inhale the necessary dose.

Nitrous oxide and ether

Great advances in chemistry in the late 18th and early 19th centuries provided medicine with the first effective anaesthetics. The gas nitrous oxide was discovered in 1772 by Joseph Priestley. In 1799 Thomas Beddoes and Humphry Davy recognized its anaesthetizing effects, but no one thought to make use of it to deaden the pain of surgery. In 1845 American chemist Charles Jackson discovered the gas ether was also an effective anaesthetic. It caused both loss of consciousness and feeling.

The first person to use anaesthetic gas for medical purposes was an American doctor named William Morton. He used ether on a patient when he extracted a tooth in 1845. The device used to deliver the gas to the patient was a surprisingly simple invention. A sealed glass jar with an air-valve contained several sponges which had been soaked in liquid ether. Connected to the jar was a long rubber tube, at the end of which was a rubber mouthpiece.

Chloroform

Ether had drawbacks, though. It had a strong, unpleasant smell, and irritated the lungs. A Scottish doctor named James Young Simpson pioneered the use of another newly discovered gas, chloroform, in 1847. It was found to be a particularly useful anaesthetic during childbirth. This met with strong opposition from religious extremists, who believed it was a woman's fate to suffer pain in childbirth. Opposition melted away, however, when Queen Victoria allowed the use of chloroform during the birth of her seventh child, Leopold.

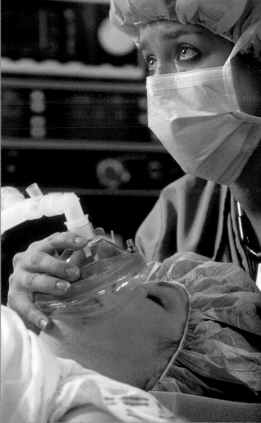

An operation today. The anaesthetist is a highly skilled specialist. She sits next to the patient, and monitors their condition via a computer display.

Today, the use of anaesthetics in surgery is a complex medical speciality, although the way anaesthetics cause loss of feeling and consciousness is still not properly understood. Highly trained doctors have a whole arsenal of gases and drugs to choose from, and monitor their patients closely throughout an operation. A patient who is to undergo a major operation may have nitrous oxide gas to induce a loss of sensation, and barbiturate and neuro-blocker drugs to induce sleep and muscle relaxation.

1799	1845	1846	1847	1853
THOMAS BEDDOES AND HUMPHRY DAVY DISCOVER NITROUS OXIDE GAS HAS AN ANAESTHETIZING EFFECT	ETHER GAS USED BY WILLIAM MORTON DURING TOOTH EXTRACTION	ETHER GAS USED BY WILLIAM MORTON DURING OPERATION TO EXTRACT A TUMOUR	CHLOROFORM GAS USED AS AN ANAESTHETIC BY JAMES YOUNG SIMPSON	QUEEN VICTORIA ACCEPTS CHLOROFORM DURING CHILDBIRTH, AND POPULARIZES ITS USE

Syringe, 1853

Like the scalpel, the syringe is an invention which is instantly associated with medicine. Giving **vaccinations**, taking blood samples, administering **anaesthetics** or painkillers – all of these medical procedures are done with a syringe.

Syringes are simple pumps. They have an air-tight plunger that moves up and down inside a chamber. At one end is a handle to move the plunger, and at the other is a hollow needle attached to a small, rigid tube. When the plunger is drawn back, this creates a **vacuum** inside the chamber which can suck liquid into the syringe. When the plunger is pushed down, liquid is forced out through the needle.

Who invented it?

The invention of the syringe had its origins in the 17th century. In 1657 two British scientists, Christopher Wren and Robert Boyle, invented syringe-type devices in their experiments with vacuums. Also around this time a French army surgeon, named Dominique Anel, invented a syringe-like device which used suction to clean the wounds of injured soldiers. The first syringe to resemble the type we use today was invented by a French physician, named Charles Pravaz, in 1853. His syringe was made of silver and could hold a cubic centimetre of liquid. Later in the century glass became the preferred material for making syringes. It was easier to clean, and a doctor could see at a glance how much liquid was inside it.

A collection of 19th-century silver and glass syringes. Today syringes are made of plastic and used only once.

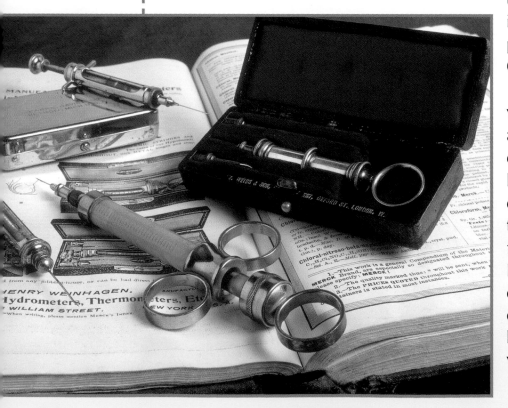

Today, syringes are made of clear plastic and are usually used just once and then thrown away. This is because diseases such as acquired immune deficiency syndrome (AIDS) can be passed on through contact with an infected person's blood.

Other methods

These days, there are other ways of injecting vaccines and medicines directly into the body. The 'microneedle', a small patch containing 400 tiny needles, is so small that it pierces the skin without reaching the nerve endings that register pain. The 'hypospray' uses pressurized helium gas to spray powdered medicine on to the skin in a form that makes it easy to absorb. Even so, the syringe and its hollow needle remain the most common way of both injecting vaccines and medicines and taking blood and other medical fluid samples.

Protecting against disease

One of the most important uses for the syringe is for vaccinations. This is a medical procedure where a person is deliberately infected with a weak form of a **virus** (called a vaccine). This then gives them **immunity** to the more deadly version of the virus. Invented in 1796 by the English doctor Edward Jenner, vaccination (also known as immunization and inoculation) has gone on to save millions of lives. It has eradicated or considerably diminished such diseases as smallpox, diphtheria, polio and tetanus.

1657	c. 1660	1853	1974
CHRISTOPHER WREN AND ROBERT BOYLE INVENT SYRINGE-TYPE VACUUM PUMPS	FRENCH SURGEON DOMINIQUE ANEL USES FORM OF SYRINGE TO CLEAN WOUNDS	FRENCH DOCTOR CHARLES PRAVAZ INVENTS MEDICAL SYRINGE	AMERICAN PHYSICIAN PHIL BROOKS INVENTS DISPOSABLE PLASTIC SYRINGE

Antiseptic spray, 1865

A patient facing an operation in early 19th-century Europe had two horrors to endure – the prospect of agonizing surgery without **anaesthetic**, and the very real possibility that the operation would kill them anyway. Those who had limbs amputated had a 50/50 chance of surviving. The severe death rate following surgery was one of medicine's major mysteries.

The reason for it was simple. In those days doctors did not know about **bacteria** and did not realize wounds could become infected. No precautions were taken to make everything clean when operating on a patient. When wounds did become infected, doctors thought the raw flesh and oozing pus were a natural part of the healing process.

A Hungarian doctor named Ignaz Semmelweis was the first person to offer a solution. He realized that infections could be carried by doctors and nurses from one patient to another. He insisted that medical staff regularly clean their hands with disinfectant. Although this procedure was very effective it was not immediately accepted by his fellow medics.

Carbolic acid

Someone who did pick up on Semmelweis's ideas, though, was a British surgeon named Joseph Lister. He had also studied the work of French scientist Louis Pasteur who had recently proved that invisible bacteria were the cause of infection. Lister had noted how effectively the chemical cleaner carbolic acid had reduced infections among cattle. This was the germ-killer he decided to use himself.

Lister insisted on a rigorous antiseptic (germ-killing) routine on his wards and during his operations. Instruments, dressings and wounds were all thoroughly cleaned. Most important of all was an antiseptic spray he devised, which was directed over the patient and operating table. Looking like an intricate piece of laboratory equipment, it consisted of a water heater and carbolic acid container. Water was heated to boiling point and the steam this produced was mixed with the carbolic acid. The result was a highly effective antiseptic mist which immediately led to a three-fold drop in lethal post-operative infections.

Spreading the word

Lister published articles about his antiseptic techniques in the widely-read British medical magazine *The Lancet*. Slowly but surely his ideas were adopted throughout the world. Lister's spray, and his equally important cleansing of intruments and dressings, made surgery so much safer that by the time he died, the number of operations being performed in British hospitals had gone up by one thousand per cent.

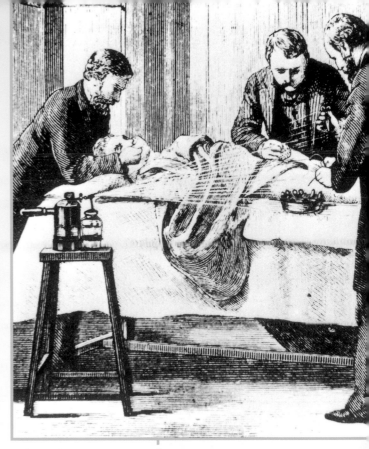

A carbolic acid spray. Messy and unpleasant to work under, it nevertheless saved countless lives by preventing infection during operations.

Prevention is better

Antiseptics have drawbacks – they may kill bacteria, but they also irritate skin. Carbolic sprays were messy and unpleasant to work with. So, towards the end of the 19th century, surgeons began to think that preventing bacteria from getting into the wound in the first place was the way forward. All equipment and the operating room should be as sterile (germ-free) as possible. Rather than just cleaned, instruments were boiled to kill any bacteria on them. This is the way surgeons work today. They even wear masks to prevent bacteria from their breath reaching their patients.

1847	1865	1886	1900
IGNAZ SEMMELWEIS INTRODUCED ANTISEPTIC PROCEDURES TO HIS MATERNITY WARD IN VIENNA	BRITISH SURGEON JOSEPH LISTER USES CARBOLIC ACID SPRAY DURING HIS OPERATIONS	STEAM STERILIZATION OF DRESSINGS INTRODUCED	USE OF STERILE RUBBER GLOVES DURING SURGERY INTRODUCED

Teeth braces, 1880

Teeth seem to be a never-ending source of discomfort for humans. Quite apart from the agony of an **abscess** or toothache, and the dread of the dentist's drill, there is a whole world of problems in the way teeth grow. Too many teeth, or teeth growing in odd positions in the jaw is called malocclusion. This condition can cause anything from an unsightly smile to a swollen, deformed face.

Adults are supposed to have 32 teeth, spaced regularly throughout the top and bottom jaw. They should all be aligned in such a way that they fit together neatly when the jaw closes. Many of us are lucky enough to have such a set of teeth, but for those who don't, American dentist Norman W Kingsley invented a branch of dentistry called orthodontics. (The word comes from the Greek *orthos* – straight – and Latin *dens* – tooth.)

Kingsley was a talented all-rounder. As well as being a dentist, he was a writer, artist and sculptor. His book *Treatise on Oral Deformities*, published in 1880, led to him being described as 'the father of orthodontics'.

These fixed braces use metal brackets cemented to each tooth with a wire threaded through each bracket. They are difficult to remove and can be uncomfortable at first.

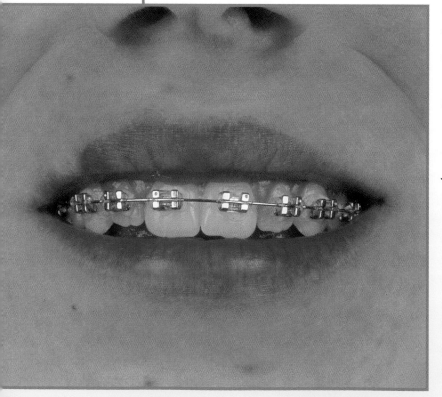

Other American dentists at the time also made major contributions to this new branch of dentistry. As well as writing a highly influential book *A Treatise on the Irregularities of the Teeth...*, J N Farrar designed the first recognizably modern teeth braces. These applied a constant, mild pressure to teeth, to gently change their position in the jaw. Finally, Edward H Angle went on to found the first school of orthodontics at the turn of the 20th century.

Space-age braces

The first braces were ugly, unpleasant looking devices. They had heavy metal plates which were anchored to teeth with dental cement, and clumsy thick wires connecting them together. Some braces even had wiring that protruded from the mouth, and must have made the wearer feel very self-conscious. These days, braces are made of high-tech plastics and metals, some of which were developed by the NASA space programme. The wires that slowly pull the teeth into position are stronger and more flexible, and are activated by body heat. Braces today are altogether more comfortable to wear. They also work more effectively, which cuts down on the time the patient has to wear them. For the daringly fashionable, some braces are even available in bold, bright colours!

American dentists were the pioneers in this branch of dentistry, so it seems fitting that America is the country where teeth braces are most common. Today, over four million American and Canadian children (and even some adults) wear braces in any given year.

Braces today. Space-age technology allows light, strong and comfortable braces that work more quickly and efficiently. They are made of material that blends with the colour of the teeth and are much easier to remove than earlier braces.

1880	1901	1907
NORMAN W KINGSLEY PUBLISHES *TREATISE ON ORAL DEFORMITIES*	AMERICAN SOCIETY OF ORTHODONTIA FOUNDED	FIRST ORTHODONTIC JOURNAL PUBLISHED

Contact lenses, 1887

Scientists have long known that light is altered when it passes through water in a glass, or through a glass **lens**, and that this can be used to aid people with poor eyesight. As early as the 5th century, reading stones – glass spheres placed in front of objects – were used to help people see better. Glasses were invented in the late 13th century and have since become invaluable to people with poor eyesight, yet, even the best ones have disadvantages. Peripheral (side) vision is poor, and they can get steamed up or wet and blurred. They are inconvenient if you want to play sport, and some people feel less attractive when they are wearing them.

Leonardo and Descartes

Early contact lenses may have freed people from the inconvenience of wearing glasses, but they were difficult to get used to and hard on the eyes.

Contact lenses, which sit directly on the eye, came a whole 600 years after glasses were invented. Renaissance genius Leonardo da Vinci is often credited with coming up with the idea. He was said to have stuck his head in a glass bowl of water and noticed how this improved his eyesight. He knew that the bowl and water were acting like a lens. In 1508, inspired by this experiment, he made sketches of small, water-filled lenses that were meant to sit directly on the eye. The French philosopher and scientist René Descartes made similar sketches. Neither made a working model of their idea.

From glass to plastic

The first practical contact lenses were made in 1887 by a German optician named Adolf E Fick. These were developed to correct astigmatism (distorted vision) rather than to enable the wearer to stop wearing glasses. Made of ground glass, they were so uncomfortable they could be worn only for a short time.

In 1938 a German company called Obrig and Muller made a major breakthrough when they developed plastic lenses. These were much lighter and therefore more comfortable to wear. They were much bigger than today's contact lenses and covered most of the front of the eyeball. Another breakthrough came in 1948, when American Kevin Touhy devised plastic lenses that were small enough just to sit on the cornea (the front of the eye, containing the iris and pupil). These were much more comfortable.

During the 1950s and 60s Czech scientist Otto Wichterle devised soft plastic lenses which were first sold in 1971 by the ophthalmic company Bausch and Lomb. They were even more comfortable than the previous plastic lenses but were easy to damage and much more difficult to clean.

Expensive alternative

Today, contact lenses are a popular alternative to glasses, although they are generally more expensive to buy. The inconvenience of cleaning can even be avoided – with disposable lenses, which are worn once, and then thrown away. These were first sold in 1997, by the pharmaceutical company Johnson and Johnson. Disposable contact lenses cost around one pound a day – £365 a year – which is maybe twice the cost of a good pair of glasses, which could last for several years.

1508	1887	1938	1971	1997
LEONARDO DA VINCI DRAWS SKETCHES OF WATER-FILLED LENSES WHICH SIT ON THE EYE	ADOLF E FICK INVENTS FIRST GLASS CONTACT LENSES	PLASTIC LENSES DEVELOPED BY OBRIG AND MULLER	SOFT LENSES INTRODUCED AND RAPIDLY BECOME VERY POPULAR	ONE-DAY DISPOSABLE LENSES INTRODUCED

X-ray machine, 1895

Fate can play funny tricks on inventors. The man who invented the microscope failed to understand how useful it could be. The man who invented antiseptics was dismissed from his job for encouraging his colleagues to use them. Several decades passed before their use became common practice. Wilhelm Roentgen, however, received immediate recognition for his invention – the X-ray machine – yet he stumbled across it by accident.

Roentgen was a German physicist working at the University of Würzberg. His area of research was electricity and its effects on gas-filled and **vacuum** tubes. One day in November 1895 he was passing a high voltage through a vacuum tube when he noticed it sent out visible rays. Experiments revealed that these rays would leave traces on a photographic plate. Even more curiously, they could pass through solid objects like a box or a hand and make an image of what lay inside. He named these – X-rays (X, being the standard scientific term for something unknown).

This is one of the first ever X-rays. It shows the structure of the bones in Roentgen's wife's hand. A ring can clearly be seen on her third finger. Today, X-rays are commonplace, but in the late 19th century images such as this seemed almost miraculous.

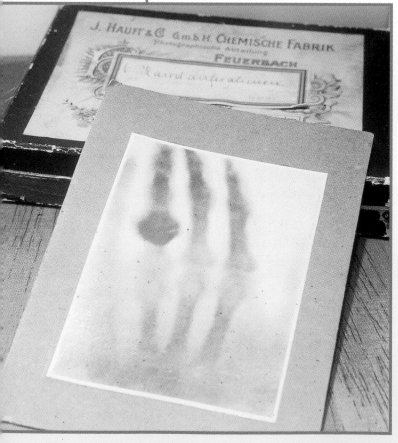

Roentgen instantly recognized these rays could be of immense use to medicine. Barely weeks after his first experiments his invention was reported all over the world. Within three years X-ray machines were being widely used by doctors.

Seeing inside the body

X-rays had a multitude of uses. They could show broken or diseased bones, decay in teeth, blocked arteries, fluid on the lungs and **tumours**. Making a **diagnosis** became much easier. Surgeons now knew exactly what they were looking for before they operated. X-rays had made a radical difference in the world of medicine.

Bones and foreign objects within the body showed up best of all in X-ray photographs. Soft body **organs** such as the stomach and intestine were much more difficult to see but in 1897 American physician Walter Cannon devised a 'bismuth meal' which could be swallowed. It coated the stomach and intestines, and showed them clearly on X-ray plates. This method is still used, although patients now swallow a chemical mix called barium sulphate, which is safer and more palatable.

Healing X-rays

It was soon discovered that X-rays could also be used to treat skin diseases and **cancer**. Although they can have unpleasant side effects, they are still used to treat cancer today.

Today, X-ray film is much more sensitive than the plates used in the earliest experiments. A low-dose X-ray reveals a clear image on film in barely a second. Even so, you will notice that radiologists (doctors and nurses who work with X-rays) still leave the room whenever they make an X-ray. You are not in danger from the dose you get, but too much exposure to X-rays is harmful. If the radiologists stayed in the room they would be exposed to X-rays all day.

The most sophisticated X-ray machines used today are called CAT (Computer Axial Tomography) scanners. They take a whole series of X-rays and produce a detailed three-dimensional image for doctors to study.

How a body scanner works
A modern computer axial tomography (CAT) scanner, which can produce three-dimensional images of the inside of the body. A patient must lie very still on the couch for up to 30 minutes. A computer puts together all the information, which can then be studied on a video screen.

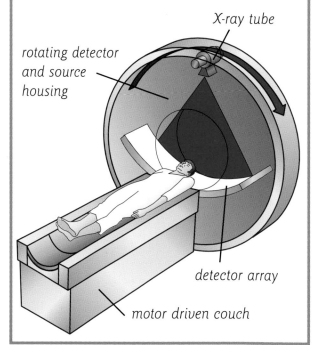

X-ray tube

rotating detector and source housing

detector array

motor driven couch

1895	1897	1901	1914	1975
WILHELM ROENTGEN DISCOVERS X-RAYS	WALTER CANNON DEVISES 'BISMUTH MEAL' TO MAKE SOFT BODY TISSUE VISIBLE TO X-RAYS	WILHELM ROENTGEN AWARDED NOBEL PRIZE FOR PHYSICS	X-RAY MACHINES IN COMMON USE AROUND THE WORLD	CAT SCANS (3-D X-RAYS) INTRODUCED TO HOSPITALS

Portable electric hearing aid, 1923

For thousands of years the most common way of coping with hearing loss was to use some form of ear trumpet. This was a tube with a large opening at one end which caught incoming sounds and **transmitted** them to a small earpiece at the other end of the tube. You can get some idea of how effective they were by cupping your hands behind your ears. You will instantly be aware that background sounds are louder, and that you can hear noises you had not previously noticed.

The earliest known types of ear trumpet were made of the hollowed-out horn of a cow or ram. Over the centuries people experimented with various other types of material, such as wood, brass, silver and shell. In the early 19th century one of the most elaborate ear trumpets ever, was made for the Portuguese king, John VI. He had a throne made with arm rests in the shape of snarling lions' heads. Courtiers knelt and spoke into the lions' mouths and the sound was carried by tubes into the king's ears.

The first portable electric hearing aid – the Otophone. Very different from the tiny hearing aids of today, the Otophone weighed 7 kilograms and had to be carried around in a small case!

Hearing through teeth

One hearing aid, used in the late 19th century, was called the Dentaphone. It was shaped like a fan and held in the teeth. The wearer leaned forward to catch the sound of someone speaking to them. The vibrations of the voice were caught by the fan and transmitted through the teeth to the skull and the ear. It worked well enough to become a common hearing aid in Victorian times.

Hidden aids

Other Victorian hearing devices tried to be more discreet. One consisted of a table with an urn of flowers. Hidden in the flowers was a large horn. A tube from the horn led through the urn and table out to the side, where the deaf person would listen to the conversation with a small earpiece. It was not a success. The listener had to be sitting down to use it, and the person speaking to them had to shout into the flowers. Other Victorian aids included ear trumpets concealed in top hats and even tiaras!

Telephone and radio

In the late 19th century the famous inventor Alexander Graham Bell was experimenting with hearing devices for deaf children when he came up with the telephone. Another inventor, Miller Reese Hutchinson, made use of Bell's ideas and invented the first electric hearing aid in 1901. He called it the Telephone Transmitter. It had a microphone to catch sound and turn it into an electrical signal, an amplifier to make the signal stronger and an earpiece which turned the signal back into sound.

These, and other similar devices, were as cumbersome and awkward to use as the previous non-electric ear trumpets. The real breakthrough came in 1923, when the Marconi company invented the Otophone. It was packed into a case weighing 7 kilograms, but was small and light enough to be carried around.

Today, miniature hearing aids use **microchip** and **digital** technology. They are so small they can be worn inside the ear canal and adjusted by remote control.

1901	1920	1923	1935	1952
MILLER REESE HUTCHINSON INVENTS THE FIRST ELECTRIC HEARING AID	EARL CHARLES HANSON'S VACTUPHONE USES VALVE TECHNOLOGY	MARCONI INTRODUCE THE OTOPHONE, THE FIRST PORTABLE ELECTRIC HEARING AID	A. EDWIN STEVEN DEVELOPS ELECTRIC HEARING AID SMALL ENOUGH TO BE WORN ON THE BODY	SONOTONE PRODUCE THE FIRST TRANSISTORIZED HEARING AID, WHICH CAN BE WORN DISCREETLY BEHIND THE EAR

Iron lung, 1928

Imagine being trapped inside a coffin-sized iron box, with only your head poking out of the end. As you lie there, leather bellows wheeze up and down relentlessly, forcing air in and out. It sounds like a nightmare, but for many children in the mid-20th century it was a lifesaver. The box, called the 'iron lung' by a journalist, helped people who could no longer breathe, to stay alive.

In the first half of the 20th century, a **virus** called **polio** claimed thousands of lives. It lurked in contaminated food or water, and paralysed the nerves that controlled the limbs or lungs. If the lungs were affected, the victim could suffocate within hours. Children were particularly vulnerable to polio, which made it one of the most feared diseases of the age. What was needed was some sort of breathing device, which could keep a child alive for a few vital days, until the effects of the virus wore off and they could breathe again.

Cat in a box

In 1926, American charitable foundation the Rockerfeller Institute began research into ways of saving polio victims. A member of the team was physician Philip Drinker. His brother was researching the way animals breathe. As part of this research he constructed a sealed box to place a cat in, to observe how much air it breathed in and out.

Drinker realized a similar device could actually help people to breathe.

He had a box built that was large enough for a human and used a modified **vacuum** cleaner to pump air in and out of it. When air was pumped out, this caused a person's chest to rise and air was drawn into the lungs. When air was pumped in, the chest fell and air was expelled from the lungs.

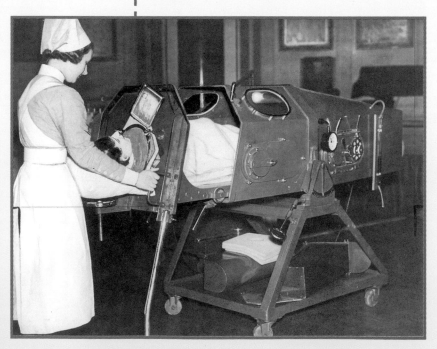

A young victim of polio inside an iron lung. A rubber seal around the patient's neck kept the iron box air-tight.

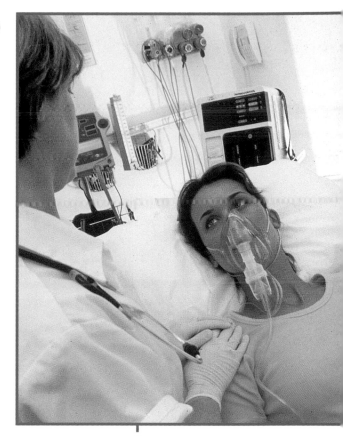

Saving lives

In 1928 Drinker's device was tried out on an unconscious eight-year-old girl who could barely breathe and was near to death. She regained consciousness within minutes and was soon asking for ice-cream. The iron lung obviously worked, although its first patient died soon afterwards of **pneumonia**. By 1931 the iron lung was being produced commercially and became a common sight in hospitals all over the world.

Breathing apparatus today – oxygen is received via a face mask, with as little discomfort to the patient as possible.

Today, a face mask and a small ventilator is used to help patients suffering from serious breathing disorders. Only a few hospitals still have iron lungs. However, between the 1930s and the 1950s these clumsy and rather sinister-looking devices saved thousands of lives.

1832	1881	1928	1931 ONWARDS	1954
JOHN DALZIEL FIRST SUGGESTS IDEA OF SEALED BOX TO HELP PATIENTS WITH BREATHING DIFFICULTIES	ALEXANDER GRAHAM BELL DESIGNS 'VACUUM JACKET'	PHILIP DRINKER INVENTS 'IRON LUNG'	IRON LUNGS SOLD ALL OVER THE WORLD	FIRST SUCCESSFUL POLIO VACCINE INTRODUCED

Electron microscope, 1933

The invention of the microscope in 1590 brought huge advances in medicine over the next three centuries. It was an essential tool in the discovery of **bacteria** that caused diseases, yet, even today, the most powerful ordinary microscopes can only magnify up to 2500 times. By the early 20th century scientists were wondering how they could see into the even smaller dimensions of the microscopic world.

A German scientist named Ernst Ruska came up with the answer. In 1933 he devised a magnifying device called an electron microscope. An ordinary microscope uses **lenses** and light to examine an object. Ruska's microscope used a stream of electrons – tiny particles that are part of **atoms**. These electrons bounced off the object being examined and on to a detector, which used the information to make an image on a TV screen.

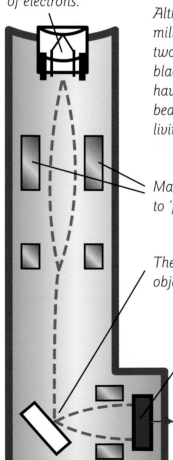

An electron gun makes a stream of electrons.

Magnets are used like lenses to 'focus' the electrons.

The electrons hit the object being studied.

They bounce off it onto this detector screen.

The screen translates the signals it receives on to a computer screen.

How an electron microscope works

*Although they can magnify as much as a million times, electron microscopes have two drawbacks. Firstly, they only produce black and white images, which have to have colour added. Secondly, the electron beam only works in a **vacuum**. Nothing living can ever be examined by one.*

At first Ruska's invention could only magnify up to ten times – around the same amount as Zacharias Jansen's first microscope. It soon improved however and within a year, Ruska's microscope was magnifying images thousands of times greater than an ordinary microscope could achieve. In 1938 the Siemens electronic company began to sell the electron microscope commercially. Another medical breakthrough was just around the corner.

Mysterious germs

Ordinary microscopes had revealed that diseases such as **pneumonia** and **bronchitis** were caused by particular bacteria. However, the germs which brought on other illnesses, such as measles and rabies, could still not be found. This is because they were caused by **viruses** – sometimes a million times smaller than bacteria and the smallest living things known to science. Using an electron microscope, scientists soon discovered these deadly microkillers. Once they knew what they were dealing with, they could devise medicines to fight the viruses.

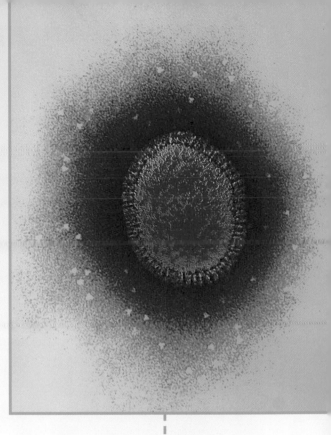

This electron microscope picture shows flu viruses. The image is magnified around 137,000 times.

Electron microscopes have proved invaluable in other areas of medical research too. Like ordinary microscopes, they provide scientists with vital clues to the life processes of the body. An image from an electron microscope also helped scientists Francis Crick and James Watson to make one of the most important discoveries of the 20th century – the structure of **DNA**, the material which makes up our **genes**.

Today, the electron microscope is just one of the tools used by medical research scientists. Scanning tunnelling microscopes have a minute needle that records changes in electric currents between the needle and the surface being examined. In other microscopes, sound waves, X-rays, magnetic forces or minute changes in temperature build up information which is then shown as an image on a computer screen.

1590	1933	1938	1953	1981
LIGHT MICROSCOPE INVENTED	ERNST RUSKA INVENTS ELECTRON MICROSCOPE	SIEMENS ELECTRONIC COMPANY SELL THE ELECTRON MICROSCOPE COMMERCIALLY	ELECTRON MICROSCOPE IMAGES HELP FRANCIS CRICK AND JAMES WATSON DISCOVER STRUCTURE OF DNA	SCANNING TUNNELLING MICROSCOPE PERFECTED

Genetic engineering, 1973

The health of every person on the planet is closely connected to their **genes** – complex sets of chemical instructions in body **cells**, made up of a substance called **DNA**. Humans have around 30,000 genes. They instruct the body how to build itself and how to act. They decide how tall someone is, for example, and whether they are likely to develop a particular illness such as **cancer**.

In 1953 Briton Francis Crick and American James Watson discovered the structure of DNA. Once this structure was understood, scientists could then set about inventing ways to change genes in living things. This is called **genetic engineering** and it is likely to have a major effect on all aspects of medicine.

The 'double helix' of DNA looks like a spiral staircase. It contains sequences of four particular proteins which make up a chemical code for each of the body's genes.

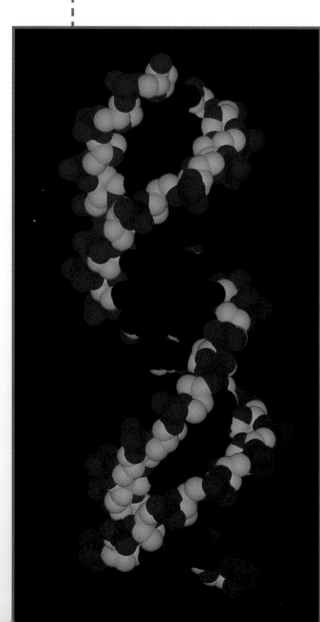

How it began

In 1973 American biochemists Stanley Cohen and Herbert Boyer took the first steps in genetic engineering when they cut a strand of **bacteria** DNA at a specific point and inserted a gene from another living thing into it.

In the world of medicine, genetic engineering allows scientists to invent new types of plants and animals that can be used to treat illness. For example, a type of bacteria has been engineered that produces the drug insulin, which diabetics need to stay alive.

The entire sequence of every one of the human body's genes (called the genome) has also been recorded. This will have a huge impact on scientists' understanding of how to detect and cure illness.

Therapy

Research is currently being carried out on the introduction of specific genes into the body to cure illnesses such as cystic fibrosis (where the lungs become clogged up with mucus). This is called gene therapy. Scientists are also investigating the possibility of curing inherited diseases, such as sickle cell anaemia, by altering the genetic make-up of people who carry the genes that cause these illnesses. This is called germline therapy.

Genetic engineering is still a very young science and many of its most recent breakthroughs are yet to have an impact on medicine. At the time of writing, the possibilities seem endless, but only time will tell whether genetic engineering lives up to its promises.

Differences in healthy and unhealthy genes show up as different colours and shades on a computer screen. These genes are unhealthy so are brighter in colour than they would be if they were healthy.

Cloning

In 1996 scientists in Scotland **cloned** a sheep, which they named Dolly. They did this by taking a body cell from an adult sheep and using its DNA to make an exact copy of that sheep. In the future cloning could allow scientists to produce tailor-made body **organs** for transplant patients, or create whole herds of cows or sheep that produce useful drugs in their milk. The technique could also be used to enable infertile couples to have a child who would be a clone of one of them.

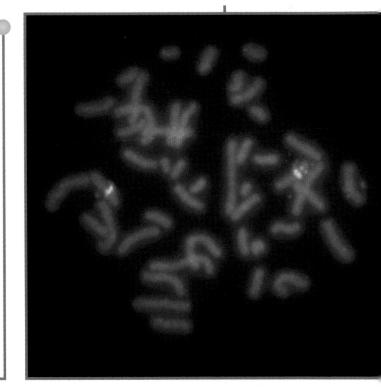

1953	1973	1986	1990	1996	2000
FRANCIS CRICK AND JAMES WATSON DISCOVER THE STRUCTURE OF DNA	STANLEY COHEN AND HERBERT BOYER CARRY OUT FIRST GENETIC ENGINEERING WITH BACTERIA	HUMAN GENOME PROJECT SET UP TO LIST SEQUENCE OF ENTIRE HUMAN GENOME	FIRST TRIALS FOR 'GENE THERAPY'	DOLLY, A CLONED SHEEP, CREATED BY ROSLIN INSTITUTE, SCOTLAND	FIRST DRAFT OF HUMAN GENOME PUBLISHED

MRI scanner, 1977

Although X-ray pictures are extraordinary things – especially three-dimensional CAT scans – they can only see so much. Right from the start, it was clear that X-rays would always show up solid parts of the body, such as bones, much better than softer parts. Medical scientists are always searching for better ways of seeing inside the body and in 1977 another major breakthrough was made. The Magnetic Resonance Imaging (MRI) scanner was invented.

American Raymond Damadian led the team which built the scanner. Like an X-ray machine, it can look into the body and 'see' bones but it is especially good at showing softer tissue such as the brain, or body tissue inside bones, such as the spinal column. It is not so good at examining the heart or lungs, as their movement blurs the image the scanner produces.

History

The origins of the MRI scanner go back to 1945 when scientists discovered that **atoms** in an object placed inside a magnetic field give off signals called radio waves. They called this phenomenon nuclear magnetic resonance (NMR). In the 1950s an NMR researcher named Felix Bloch stuck his finger in the laboratory apparatus and discovered it gave off a strong signal. Bloch quickly realized that NMR could be used to examine the insides of people's bodies. In 1971, building on this research, Damadian used NMR apparatus to detect a **tumour** in a **cancer** patient. The idea worked so well he went on to build a scanner capable of examining a whole body. The scanner looks like a big box with a hole in the middle for the patient to lie in, and uses powerful magnets to produce radio signals in the body. It can detect these signals and turn them into an image on a TV screen.

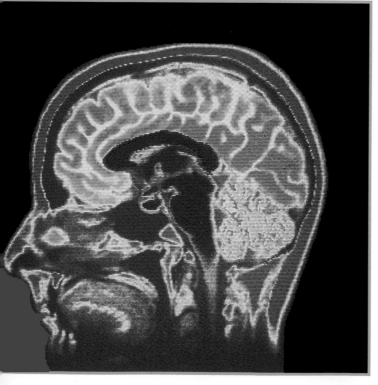

A patient's head seen by a MRI scanner. In this image you can clearly see the brain, the airway passage inside the nose, and the tongue.

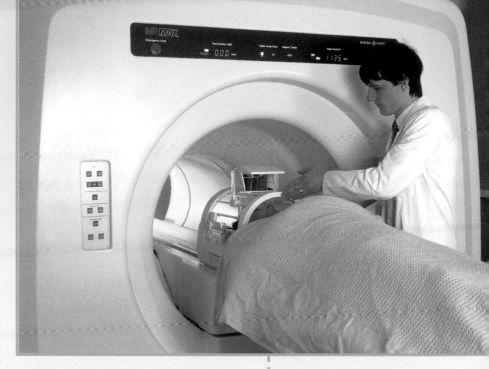

Harmless

Unlike X-rays, which expose the body to harmful **radioactivity** (albeit in very small doses) the MRI scanner seems to be completely harmless and pain-free. It also produces almost instant images. It does have disadvantages for a patient, though. Being placed inside a scanner, which makes alarming clanking noises, can be quite a claustrophobic experience. The scanning process can also take anything from 30 to 60 minutes, during which the patient must lie completely still. Because very strong magnets are used patients with metal clips or devices inside their body, such as a heart pacemaker, cannot be examined.

MRI scanners are painless to the patient, although some people find being in one can be quite a claustrophobic experience.

Other scanners

Aside from X-rays and MRI, there are other ways of looking inside the body. One method, called positron emission tomography (PET), introduces a mild radioactive substance into a patient, which is then picked up by a scanner. This is particularly useful for examining digestive **organs** such as the stomach. Another technique is called ultrasound. This makes a picture on a TV screen by detecting sound waves inside a person.

1945	1971	1977	1984
NUCLEAR MAGNETIC RESONANCE DISCOVERED	RAYMOND DAMADIAN USES NMR APPARATUS TO DETECT A TUMOUR	FIRST MRI SCANNER BUILT, IT CAN PRODUCE A WHOLE BODY IMAGE	MRI SCANNERS APPROVED FOR USE IN MEDICINE AND SOLD TO HOSPITALS ALL AROUND THE WORLD

Endoscope and camera, 1982

Despite huge advances in effectiveness and safety, the business of making an opening in a body to perform surgery is always uncomfortable and risky. Recently, however, medical scientists have developed techniques that allow a surgeon to operate inside a patient with only the smallest **incision** being made. This is called keyhole surgery and it has come about thanks to an invention called the endoscope – a tube used to look inside the human body.

The first endoscope dates from 1806, when an Austrian physician named Philip Bozzini built a device he called the 'Lichtleiter'. A candle was used to provide illumination, but the device was never used on people. Over the next few decades the idea was developed further, but only really came into its own with the arrival of **fibre-optic** technology.

A keyhole surgery camera in action. The surgeon can see what he needs to do on the TV monitor.

In 1930, a German medical student named Heinrich Lamm suggested using glass fibres to examine the inside of the human body. His idea was ahead of its time. The glass used in the 1930s was too poor in quality to give a good image. Improvements in the quality after the Second World War led to the development of glass-fibre endoscopes in the 1960s.

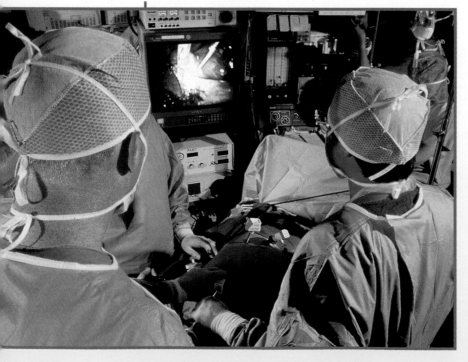

Adding a camera

In 1982 a miniature camera was fitted to an endoscope. This let surgeons see what they were doing by looking at a video monitor, rather than peering into the eyepiece of the endoscope. It also allowed what they saw to be recorded on video tape. In 1996 a live operation was 'broadcast' over the Internet, using such a camera.

Fibre optics

The idea of fibre optics – thin rods of glass which carry light – came about in the 1840s when it was noticed that light bent along the curve of water in a fountain. The idea was developed over the century and in 1900 it was put to practical use with a forerunner of the modern endoscope. This was a curved quartz rod, which was used in dentistry to light up the inside of the mouth. In the 1960s and 70s very pure glass fibres were developed, which could carry light over long distances with very little loss or distortion. Today, millions of miles of fibre-optic cables carry Internet, telephone and television signals all around the world. A single fibre can carry 200 television channels and 200,000 phone conversations.

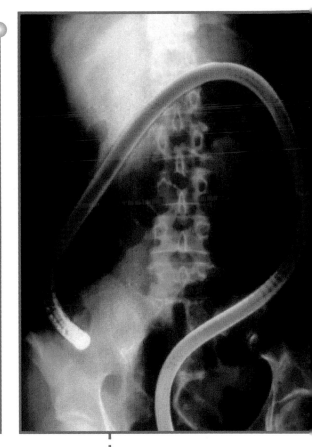

This coloured X-ray shows an endoscope inside a patient's **abdomen**. *The bones of the spine can also be seen (in green).*

Today, endoscopes are a vital part of a surgeon's examination and operating equipment. Most endoscopes hold two fibre-optic tubes, which run from one end to the other. One tube carries light into the body, the other has a **lens** at one end, which carries the image of what the endoscope is pointed at.

Doctors use an endoscope to examine such areas as the inside of the nose and the digestive system. The endoscope also allows doctors to carry out surgery by making an opening in the body only 1–2 centimetres wide. Some endoscopes even have their own miniature surgical instruments attached to them. One recent use of the endoscope is to send a **laser** beam down it to burn away **tumours** or repair body tissue.

1806	1930	1960s	1982	1996
PHILIP BOZZINI BUILDS FIRST ENDOSCOPE	HEINRICH LAMM SUGGESTED USING GLASS FIBRES FOR MEDICAL EXAMINATION	FIRST USE OF GLASS-FIBRE ENDOSCOPES	MINIATURE CAMERA FITTED TO ENDOSCOPE	LIVE OPERATION 'BROADCAST' ON INTERNET, USING CAMERA IN ENDOSCOPE

Timeline

10,000BC	First evidence of surgery
3000BC	Sumerians develop copper scalpel
c. 2000BC	First known use of acupuncture needles
c. 700BC	First known false teeth
13th century AD	First spectacles made from glass **lenses**
1508	Leonardo da Vinci draws sketches of water-filled lenses which sit on the eye
1536	Ambroise Paré invents artificial limbs
1590	Zacharias Jansen makes first microscope
1667	First successful animal-to-human blood transfusion by Jean-Baptiste Denis
1770	Porcelain false teeth invented
1818	First successful human-to-human blood transfusion by James Blundell
1819	First use of stethoscope by Laënnec
1845	Ether gas used by William Morton as an **anaesthetic** during tooth extraction
1847	Chloroform gas used as an anaesthetic by James Young Simpson
1853	Charles Pravaz invents medical syringe
1861	Louis Pasteur proves that **bacteria** cause illness
1865	Joseph Lister uses carbolic acid spray during operations

1880	Norman W Kingsley publishes *Treatise on Oral Deformities*
1887	Adolf E Fick invents glass contact lenses
1895	Wilhelm Roentgen discovers X-rays
1900	Sterile rubber gloves first used during surgery
1901	Miller Reese Hutchinson invents the electric hearing aid
1923	Marconi introduce first portable electric hearing aid
1928	Philip Drinker invents 'iron lung'
1933	Ernst Ruska invents electron microscope
1953	Francis Crick and James Watson discover the structure of **DNA**
1954	First successful **polio** vaccine introduced
1960s	First use of **fibre-optic** endoscopes
1973	Stanley Cohen and Herbert Boyer carry out first **genetic engineering**
1974	Phil Brooks invents disposable plastic syringe
1975	CAT scans introduced to hospitals
1977	First MRI scanner built
1982	Miniature camera fitted to endoscope
1996	**Cloned** sheep Dolly created by Roslin Institute, Scotland
1997	One-day disposable contact lenses introduced
2000	First draft of Human Genome Project published

Glossary

abdomen the part of the body below the chest at the front of the trunk, containing the intestines

abscess area of the body filled with pus

anaesthetic substance which causes loss of sensation in the body, especially loss of pain

asthma medical condition where a patient has difficulty in breathing, and feels tightness in the chest

atom minute particle that makes up the basic building blocks of substances

bacteria tiny organisms, many of which cause diseases

bronchitis illness which affects the lungs and causes coughing and difficulty breathing

cancer an often fatal growth in the body, caused by body cells dividing uncontrollably

cell tiny section which makes up the various parts of a plant or animal

clone living thing which is genetically identical to another living thing, because it has been produced with the same DNA

diagnosis medical term for the identification of a disease based on the examination of particular symptoms

diaphragm muscular partition between the upper body and the abdomen

digital representing information in numerical form – most often used by computers

DNA chemical code which is found in a gene

fibre-optics transmission of light down flexible, transparent tubes of glass

gear toothed wheel used in machinery to change the speed or direction of a mechanism

genes set of chemicals, passed on when living things reproduce, which determine the shape and character of their offspring

genetic engineering science of changing the shape and character of living things by altering the genes that they inherit

immunity ability of the body to fight off particular illnesses

incision cut made with a scalpel during surgery

laser machine which produces a very intense beam of hot light

lens piece of transparent material, such as glass, which can bend light and can be used to make things look bigger or clearer

lever rigid bar which is part of the mechanism of a machine. Levers usually transfer a force from one part of the machine to another.

microchip tiny piece of electrical machinery used in computers

organ particular part of the body, such as the heart, brain or liver

pneumonia disease where the lungs fill with fluid

polio disease which causes paralysis, especially in the limbs and lungs

radioactivity particles or rays given off by atoms of particular materials

rheumatism painful joints and muscles

sceptic someone who mistrusts ideas, especially new ideas

transmit pass on, often said of an illness caused by a bacteria or virus

trepanning ancient medical practice in which holes were drilled in the head, supposedly to release evil spirits which were causing an illness

tuberculosis disease which causes swellings in the lungs

tumour swelling in the body caused by an abnormal growth of cells

turbine wheel with blades inside a machine or engine, which can be rotated at very high speed (for example, by high pressure steam or water)

ulcer sore on the skin or a body organ which heals very slowly

vaccination deliberate introduction into the body of a bacteria or viruses which causes a mild form of a disease. This then gives the body immunity to the more deadly form of this disease.

vacuum space which contains nothing, not even air

virus extremely small organisms which cause illnesses

Index